The <u>ONE</u> of Power

The One of Power

The <u>ONE</u> of Power

Teamwork Skills for
Building and Managing Your
<u>ONE</u> Dream Team

Frederick Boyd & Instafo

instafo

Copyright © Instafo

All rights reserved.

It is impermissible to reproduce any part of this book without prior consent. All violations will be prosecuted to the fullest extent of the law.

While attempts have been made to verify the information contained within this publication, neither the author nor the publisher assumes any responsibility for errors, omissions, interpretation or usage of the subject matter herein.

This publication contains the opinions and ideas of its author and is intended for informational purpose only. The author and publisher shall in no event be held liable for any loss or other damages incurred from the usage of this publication.

ISBN 978-1-727-83263-1

Printed in the United States of America

First Edition

CONTENTS

Chapter 1: One's Solo Limitation

1.1 Independent Interdependency..........9

1.2 Team Player Merits..........10

1.3 Reevaluation: Collaboration Conversion..........13

Chapter 2: One's Friendly Familiarity

2.1 Barriers Breakdown..........15

2.2 Indirect Interrelation..........18

2.3 Team Exercise: Positive Attributes Exchange..........19

Chapter 3: One's Camaraderie Creation

3.1 Common Goals Mergence..........22

3.2 Member's Worth Acknowledgement..........26

3.3 Survey: Professional Drive Discovery..........27

Chapter 4: One's Communication Culture

4.1 Secret Specialized Language..........29

4.2 Linguistic Modification: Alternative Wordings..........32

Chapter 5: One's Team Tradition

5.1 Off-Work Bonding..34

5.2 Operation Eat Out..35

5.3 Budgeting Note..37

Chapter 6: One's Team-Building Activities

6.1 Activity 1: The Team's Conviction...........................39

6.2 Activity 2: The Team's Core....................................40

6.3 Activity 3: The Team's Connection.........................40

6.4 Activity 4: The Team's Codes..................................41

Chapter 7: One's Special Force

7.1 Crucial Leadership Role..43

7.2 Effective Team Management..................................44

The One of Power

The One of Power

Chapter 1:

One's Solo Limitation

Independent Interdependency

When it comes to the important things in life—planning financial matters, setting personal objectives, or gauging personal ambitions—many people believe that they can only truly rely on themselves.

This attitude may be perfectly justified, especially when there are so many issues among people regarding trust, loyalty, and professionalism.

After all, as the idiom goes, *"To thine own self be true."*

However, there is only so much that one can do for oneself. We also need to rely on other people to get things done because very few ever reach their final destination without some sort of help along the way. That is why we believe there's still a good reason to work with others—whether it's finding people with complementary skills, gaining more "hands" in order to achieve a common goal, or simply getting things done faster.

We are referring to the quest for **effective teamwork**. This does not imply "hitching your *wagon*" to everybody who crosses your personal or professional path in order to gain acceptance, or naively opening the "doors to your personal space" to people you've just met simply for the sake of collaboration.

Team Player Merits

For all of the skeptics out there, true teamwork involves neither of those things. One does not simply forsake common sense or self-preservation just to be a "**team player.**"

If done effectively, teamwork can be a win-win situation with the following merits:

- **You can combine strengths and achieve more satisfying results.** Imagine, for instance, that you are a 15th Century European navigator who wants to build a boat and sail to the Americas. You will need a diverse team to first build a craft solid enough to make the journey—your vessel must have the right measurements, the right type of timber, the right weight, etc. Also, the chances of a "crew of one" (by yourself only) making such a long and arduous journey are remote at best, so you will need a second team to serve on your crew by communicating well and executing orders.

- **You can learn from others and expand your skill set.** Through effective teamwork, you can observe others in action—their skills, abilities, and personalities—and use those examples to bolster your own ways of working. This often can be a particularly useful endeavor because you can then see what others do, compare and contrast to your own methods, and learn how the two approaches can be combined into an even better skill or approach, or learn a better way for you to do things.

- **You can create a network of peers who can help when you explore moving on to other ventures.** Remember that, while teammates are not permanent, your interaction with your teammates can be periodic in nature and called upon when needed. While professional colleagues come and go, sharing experiences and working with one another allow you to form professional/personal bonds that may transcend your current workplace.

- **You can learn how to effectively manage, and work for/with, others.** The old saying, *"There is no 'I' in* *'team'*" applies only to accomplishing a goal together. Every team has a leader at one point who directs the others toward success. Teamwork can help you develop your leadership and collaboration skills, as well as teach you how to accept delegation from others.

Reevaluation: Collaboration Conversion

You see, effective teamwork is just like the five fingers on one hand. This may sound cliched to you, but, when you think about it, this is the perfect illustration for this concept, because:

1. each finger has a role (*e.g.*, the index finger helps you press keys or buttons),
2. the fingers cannot go anywhere without the others to complete a task, just like the thumb and the index are always in proximity of the other, and

3. they work perfectly when completing a task together, like grasping something; you can only do so effectively when you use all 5 fingers.

The strategies that will be presented will help you develop better teamwork skills. But before we get into them, please answer the following questions:

- How do you define "teamwork"?

- What challenges would you experience if working in a group of individuals with different personalities? (Give 4 to 5 challenges.)

- What type of skill or positive trait would you bring to a group if you were to join one?

- Do you think you work better within a group or by yourself? *Be sure to explain why.*

Chapter 2:

One's Friendly Familiarity

Barriers Breakdown

One thing that always works within a team setting is for the individual members to engage in a type of **familiarity exercise**. This type of exercise is often practiced in schools on the first day of classes. It is used to create a comfortable atmosphere from the very beginning that helps students coexist and tears down barriers that may cause issues.

This can also be beneficial for people working within the same environment or working on the same project. It can help team members get to know each other, as well as present a more human (or familiar) side of each of the team members.

Here are the steps for this familiarity exercise:

1. Get the team together and then distribute **small pieces of paper** to each person.

2. Explain that each team member should write something they feel makes them look funny, makes them laugh, or puts them in a good mood (they should pick only one of the three). For instance, *"The thing that makes me laugh the most is…"* Items that are humorous or project a positive mood are easier to share with others, which further helps people be at ease around one another.

3. The participants will then *exchange* their pieces of paper with another teammate. Each person will read the information out loud so everyone else can share some giggles. This lightens everyone's mood and brings

out a wide range of reactions from others, which may be surprising. You might say it reveals their humanity by showing that people are more alike than they thought. For example, a person who you initially thought was closed-minded can suddenly appear friendly, sympathetic, down-to-earth, *etc.* A simple smile or laughter during the session can show a different side of a person in addition to having a positive effect on others. (*Note that a team member left without a partner because the team is made *unevenly* can be partnered with the team leader.)

4. Finally, the team leader should take notes during the exercise and come up with **nicknames** for each person after his/her information is read aloud. Then, the leader should end the game by revealing the nickname of each team member, clearly stating that the nicknames were developed after hearing the respective stories.

Indirect Interrelation

This exercise is typically fun and leads to further discussion among the team members. The team leader should also tell the team that the nicknames given should be used regularly. This will promote a stronger feeling of camaraderie where the nicknames will become "inside jokes" that only those in the inner circle will know.

However, be careful not to reveal to the team that the goal of the exercise is familiarity—this would be like a magician exposing the secrets to his greatest performance and thus destroying the magic behind it.

When dealing with adults or teenagers, such a revelation may backfire because the team members will feel like they are being forced to *"love"* or *"accept"* somebody.

Rather, state that you are engaging in a fun and unusual way to help them remember each other's names/faces, which will have an indirect benefit of creating a familiar workplace.

- For example, the team leader can announce after giving the instruction to the exercise, *"This is how you remember a teammate forever."* This will make it seem more light-hearted and beneficial to them and ensure the success of the session.

This dynamic is comparable to a court's jester trying to please a cruel king and his entourage. All it takes is the right performance to make the king let out a small laugh, so then the king can relax a bit and have a good time with his subjects. In this case, the team members represent both the king and his subjects, and the team leader is the jester who is responsible for making everyone laugh, relax, and let down their guard.

Team Exercise: Positive Attributes Exchange

Do you want to practice making people get along together?

1. Gather your team (or if you don't have a team, organize any event where people who don't know each other come together).

2. Explain the rules of the game, but not the goal.

3. Pair up team members and have them write and exchange notes. If you end up with one member without a partner because there is an *uneven number* of people, then you as team leader should pair up with that person.

4. Have everyone read the notes out loud so everybody can appreciate what is being shared (laughter, jokes, funny comments, etc.).

5. Work on coming up with nicknames for each participant while you listen to their stories. The nicknames should be simple, memorable, and playful or humorous.

6. End the session by telling the group that the purpose of the game is to help them remember each other's names and faces.

You will notice that your team members will be more relaxed around one another. And encouraging them to use nicknames during tasks will allow them to become even more comfortable working together.

Chapter 3:
One's Camaraderie Creation

Common Goals Mergence

A very effective way you can encourage members of a team to work together is to *gather the different goals* of each member then give a speech acknowledging them during the next group meeting.

These should be **professional goals**—like getting a better position within the company, going back to school to pursue a master or different degree, or taking a renewed or different focus on something learned at school or in the workplace.

Follow these steps on how to proceed with this:

1. Set up a **small survey** to inquire about each team member's professional goals. This survey should include:

- A Heading: The professional goal followed by the name of the person who is taking the survey.

- Five to seven questions to learn more about the team member:

- marital status
- job/function
- salary
- personal ambition
- reason why it's important to work in a group
- strongest characteristic
- description and background on the professional goal

2. Distribute the questionnaire to the team members and have them complete it in 10 minutes. Timing the session is important as it will *"press"* them to focus and give accurate answers.

3. Collect the surveys and thank the team members for completing it. Review the answers within 24 hours and group the goals by category.

- For instance, out of all of the team members, you may have several whose goals are to *rise in higher ranks* within the company—their category will be "promotion."

- Another group may have similar goals to *learn as much as they can* about business and run their own company one day—their category will be "experience."

- The last group could comprise team members who are just *happy to have a job* and pay their bills—their category would be "undecided."

4. Merge the categories (like those stated in the example above) into a speech that you can deliver to the team the next day. It could resemble something like the following example:

"I know that some of you hope to move up the company ladder one day, while some of you would like to open your own businesses **(this shows you care about their personal ambition)**, *and for those who are here and are just glad to be part of this team, we would like to let you know that we are here for you, and that we encourage all of you to merge your strengths together* **(this will motivate them with their ambitions)** *and really prove that you are worthy of occupying a higher rank with us, taking what you have learned here and make something greater one day* **(you are boosting their ego, thus pushing them to work with one another)**, *and lastly to prove to us that you are proud to be*

a part of that team (this encourages everyone no matter what their professional goals are)."

5. Give your speech to the team the next day (and perhaps get a standing ovation). Try to end your speech with a call to action—for example, *"Now let's get to work."*

Member's Worth Acknowledgement

Through this process, your team members will not only connect better with you as the team leader but also will get to know one another better, therefore communicating and collaborating more.

By exposing their goals (without mentioning any names), you made them feel that they were *"in the spotlight"* and gave them the desire to prove themselves to you and the rest of the team.

Think of it like being an agent or manager of a rock star who is difficult and refuses to perform. You have to find the right way to convince the star to live up to commitments by focusing on their main career goal. The rock star will then get an ego boost and feel appreciated once again (or at least just enough to perform and deliver a great show to the audience).

Survey: Professional Drive Discovery

As an exercise, elaborate a survey for your team.

1. Remember to put a **heading** (*for instance*, professional goal, followed by the participant's name).

2. Then add **5 to 7 questions** to your survey, which should include marital status, personal ambition, thoughts about working in a group, professional goal, *etc*.

3. Use the results you get from the participants to create a **speech** that will include the different types of goals you have noted from the survey.

4. Give yourself 24 hours to complete the exercise.

Chapter 4:

One's Communication Culture

Secret Specialized Language

This next strategy is based on the principle that when a small group speaks a different language in the presence of a larger group (with the latter not understanding what the people from the former are saying), the small group is often designated as being important and privileged to be able to speak this inner-circle secret language.

The small group becomes aware of the larger group's admiration, thus feeling "special."

The whole focus of this strategy is *not* about the team learning a new language, but rather using small terms, known as **team communication codes**, in order to effectively communicate with other team members.

This is how you can help to develop this effective team communication technique:

1. Gather 50 strategic words by listing categories of terms that are commonly used in your field. Remember that the **communication code** (or "**comm code**") should be something the team members identify with or can easily recognize. Let's say if you are in the *home improvement* business, words may fall under categories like lumber, cut, paints, orders, suppliers, *etc*.

2. Simplify the words linked to each category. For example, **wooden doors** can become "wodo." You can even use numbers instead of paint colors—**white** can become number one, black number two, *etc*.

3. These <u>50 words</u> (or **groups of words**) should be learned by all team members as quickly as possible because they will work with the <u>coded words</u> every day in order to communicate faster. The significance for the team to use these words is because: 1) coded words help people get more familiar with one another (hence work faster), and 2) it adds to the culture of the group within your organization.

Again, all of your team members will feel special and relate better to the rest of the team, existing in an atmosphere where it seems that only those who speak the specific coded language have the privilege to be a part of it.

Imagine you're a technician who needs another technician to back you up while working on a very difficult task. It is helpful to be guided through a series of steps, particularly one that involves codes unique to the job, because you want someone to confirm that you are doing the right thing.

Having a unique way of communicating among team members bring them closer together—in the same way when they have no other options but to prove that they are being an effective member of this "special" team by learning and using the certain codes while working together.

Beyond all this, it's about building an inseparable team's culture.

Linguistic Modification: Alternative Wordings

Try to create a series of team communication codes that fit the dynamic of your group or your organization (the words would become codes linked to the team's activity/task).

1. To keep it simple, come up with 5 or 7 categories of **expressions** that you know are specific to your activity or project.

2. Group as many as 20 words in each category (if you fall short then it's okay).

Example: If you were involved in a baking project, you would then try to come up with words such as "chobread" that would stand for **chocolate bread** which falls under the category of pastry baking (or again, if you were renovating a home, you would come up with words like number one for **white paint** which falls under the category of painting).

Chapter 5:

One's Team Tradition

Off-Work Bonding

Social bonding has been around for ages because humans crave a connection with others. The concept is often overlooked as being *off-task* because, on the surface, it doesn't involve anything professionally related toward a common work goal.

Instead, people think this type of bonding is done simply for a group of friends to have a good time.

However, these two types of interaction can coexist.

Having a **team tradition** where teammates share an experience or event presents an occasional opportunity to maintain, and even strengthen, the team bond. For example, the annual office Christmas party is a prime example within some professions of engaging colleagues in a social setting to further enhance the team.

Also, since it doesn't happen every day, teammates can get *closer* but not *too close,* keeping some professional boundaries.

A team tradition doesn't have to be anything extravagant; it can be as simple as sharing a meal together, which is exactly what we are going to recommend.

Operation Eat Out

Obviously, due to people's different tastes, dietary requirements, and moods, you should proceed in this manner:

1. Announce that the team will go out to eat together at a chosen spot every 2 weeks.

2. Mention that since you are aware of different tastes and preferences, you are going to ask about each team member's preferred food. (You may find groups of team members who prefer the same type of foods.)

3. From there, propose a number of restaurants where it should be easy for each team member to enjoy a meal together.

4. Designate someone every two weeks to choose a spot. This ensures that the type of restaurant changes when the next person chooses. For example, if pizza is the first choice, the second choice must be something different than pizza.

5. You, as the team leader, will eat with the rest of the team. The meal experience should provide the

opportunity to discuss any topic, exchange ideas, or perhaps plan how the team can work on specific tasks.

6. As the tradition progresses, people may develop a taste for something new. To that end, you may want to survey the team's food preferences again every few months to prevent the shared meal from becoming monotonous. This allows the exercise to grow into an effective "group tradition."

Budgeting Note

One last note: no matter the team dynamic, you will need to come up with a budget for the meal that allows everyone to participate.

- For example, if the team is made up of students, you can all put aside a small amount (e.g., $5 per person) every month to allow the team leader to buy snacks and drinks for a 30-minute team gathering.

So, after getting team members to write down their favorite foods and deciding on a restaurant, choose a budget that will help you build this team meal tradition every week or two. Sharing a meal definitely has the power to bring people together.

Let's now move on to some team-building exercises.

Chapter 6:

One's Team-Building Activities

Activity 1: The Team's Conviction

Create a **professional goal survey** for your team. The survey should start with a <u>heading</u> (professional goal) and the <u>name</u> of the participant.

Create 7 questions that provide information about the participant's marital status, thoughts about working within a group, professional goals, etc.

After gathering all the info, prepare a **speech** where you will acknowledge the team's common/shared professional goals. The speech is supposed to encourage everyone to unite and do their best in order to learn and grow from their experience within the group.

Activity 2: The Team's Core

Uncover 5 aspects that you believe can help a group dynamic. These could involve communication, common goals, or familiarity.

To ensure you explain why you think that these 5 aspects are important to effective teamwork, write a 50-word paragraph for each aspect.

Activity 3: The Team's Connection

Think about the **team tradition** that we recommended involving get-together meals.

- During that meal, what do you think people who work together could be talking about, and what is the reason for your answer?

- Do you feel that, as the team leader, you should encourage the team to discuss certain topics, like different challenging assignments?

- Lastly, do you feel that, as team leader, you should write notes about the effect of having a regular get-together could have on the team's performance? If so, how would you use that information?

Activity 4: The Team's Codes

Practice your ability to create a coded language that can be used in a team.

Examples:

Activity: Creating a new fashion line for teenagers.

Category of words:
Sewing/Supplies/Threads/Silk/Fittings/Sketches.

Coded words: *The Universal* (black thread), *To finalize* (to sew fabric and come up with clothes), *etc.*

Repeat this activity with the following: Coming up with a sporting event advertisement, organizing a wedding, and cooking/serving meals in an orphanage.